IT'S TIME TO EAT A RASPBERRY

It's Time to Eat a Raspberry

Walter the Educator

Silent King Books
A WhichHead Entertainment Imprint

It's Time to Eat a Raspberry is a collectible early learning book by Walter the Educator suitable for all ages belonging to Walter the Educator's Time to Eat Book Series. Collect more books at WaltertheEducator.com

USE THE EXTRA SPACE TO TAKE NOTES AND DOCUMENT YOUR MEMORIES

RASPBERRY

It's time to eat, come see what's here,

It's Time to Eat a
Raspberry

A raspberry treat that's red and clear!

Soft and tiny, round and sweet,

A perfect berry for us to eat!

From the bush where it grows so high,

Under the blue and sunny sky,

Raspberries ripen, one by one,

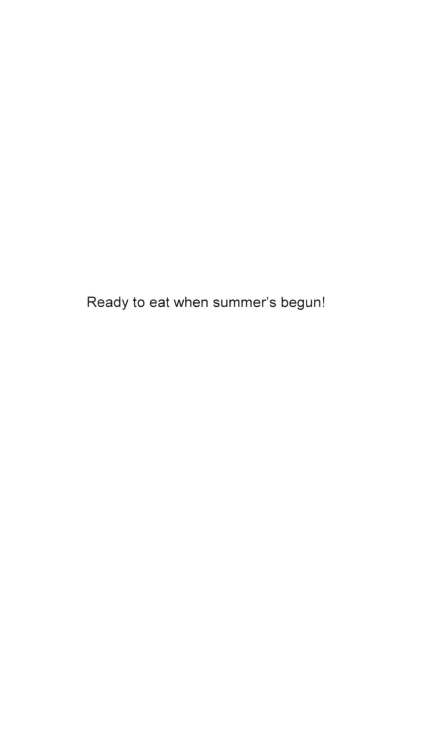

Ready to eat when summer's begun!

Oh, raspberry, tiny and bright,

You're a yummy, tasty bite!

Red and soft, a fruity cheer,

Raspberry, I'm glad you're here!

I pick you up with gentle care,

You're delicate and light as air.

Your color shines, a ruby red,

You sit so softly, like a bed.

It's Time to Eat a
Raspberry

I take a bite, what's that I find?

A burst of sweetness, pure and kind!

With a little tart, just the right mix,

You're nature's magic, full of tricks!

Oh, raspberry, tiny and bright,

You're a yummy, tasty bite!

Red and soft, a fruity cheer,

Raspberry, I'm glad you're here!

.

You're perfect in pies, in jams, and more,

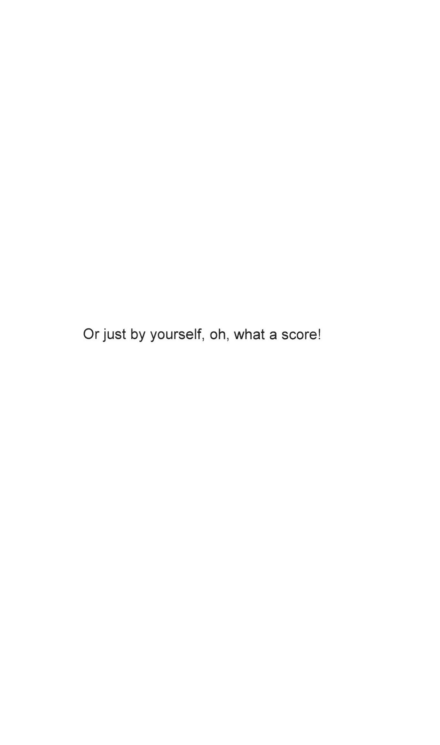

Or just by yourself, oh, what a score!

In yogurt or smoothies, you bring delight,

A raspberry snack feels just right!

Your little seeds, they add a crunch,

.

A fun surprise with every munch!

Each tiny bead is full of taste,

Not a single raspberry goes to waste!

Sometimes you're fresh, sometimes you're dried,

But every time, you bring sweet pride.

In every meal, you make it fun,

It's Time to Eat a
Raspberry

Raspberry, you're my number one!

Oh, raspberry, tiny and bright,

You're a yummy, tasty bite!

Red and soft, a fruity cheer,

Raspberry, I'm glad you're here!

ABOUT THE CREATOR

Walter the Educator is one of the pseudonyms for Walter Anderson. Formally educated in Chemistry, Business, and Education, he is an educator, an author, a diverse entrepreneur, and he is the son of a disabled war veteran. "Walter the Educator" shares his time between educating and creating. He holds interests and owns several creative projects that entertain, enlighten, enhance, and educate, hoping to inspire and motivate you. Follow, find new works, and stay up to date with Walter the Educator™

at WaltertheEducator.com